SO-AHU-106

Livonia Public Library
ALFRED NOBLE BRANCH
32901 PLYMOUTH ROAD
Livonia, Michigan 48150-1793
421-6600
LIVN #19

J629.45
M

SPACE BUSTERS

THE
SPACE RACE

Paul Mason

RAINTREE
Steck-Vaughn
PUBLISHERS

A Harcourt Company

Austin New York
www.raintreesteckvaughn.com

ALFRED NOBLE BRANCH
32901 PLYMOUTH ROAD
Livonia, Michigan 48150-1793
421-6600
LIVN #19

LOOK FOR THE ASTRONAUT

Look out for boxes like this with an astronaut in the corner. They contain extra information and amazing space buster facts and figures.

© Copyright 2002, text, Steck-Vaughn Company

All rights reserved. No part of this book may be reproduced or utilized in any form or by any means, electronic or mechanical, including photocopying, recording, or by any information storage and retrieval system, without permission in writing from the Publishers. Inquiries should be addressed to:
Copyright Permissions, Steck-Vaughn Company, P.O. Box 26015, Austin, TX 78755

Published by Raintree Steck-Vaughn Publishers, an imprint of Steck-Vaughn Company

Designer: Tessa Barwick
Editors: Susan Behar, Pam Wells
Consultant: Joyce Pope

Library of Congress Cataloging-in-Publication Data
Mason, Paul, 167-
    The space race / Paul Mason.
        p. cm.—(Space busters)
    Includes index.
    Summary: Examines mankind's exploration of outer space, from early rockets, through the competition to land on the moon first, to the cooperative efforts leading to an international space station.
    ISBN 0-7398-4851-8
    1. Space race—Juvenile literature. 2. Astronautics—United States—History—Juvenile literature. [I. Space race. 2. Astronautics—United States—History. 3. Astronautics—Soviet Union—History.] I. Title. II. Series.
TL793 .M363 2002
629.45—dc21   2001041732
Printed in Hong Kong.
Bound in the United States.
1 2 3 4 5 6 7 8 9 0 LB 05 04 03 02 01

Acknowledgments
We wish to thank the following individuals and organizations for their help and assistance and for supplying material in their collections: Camera Press 4; Corbis 3 (Bettmann), 8 bottom right (Bettmann), 9, Bettmann), 11 bottom (Dean Conger), 12 (NASA/Roger Ressmeyer), 17 (NASA), 22 (Bettmann), 26 (Hulton-Deutsch); Mary Evans Picture Library 5 bottom; MPM Images 18, 20 top, 24 main image, 25 top, 28,29, 30, 31; NASA 1, 8 top, 13, 19, 20 bottom, 21, 23 bottom; Rex Features 10, 24 inset; Science and Society Picture Library 8 bottom left (The Clarkives), 15 (NASA), 16 bottom (NASA); Science Photo Library 7 top (David A Hardy); Topham Picturepoint 5 top, 6, 7 bottom, 11 top (Tass), 16 top (Novosti), 23 top, 25 bottom, 27. Artwork by Alex Pang.

▼ This odd-looking vehicle was designed to land humans on the Moon.

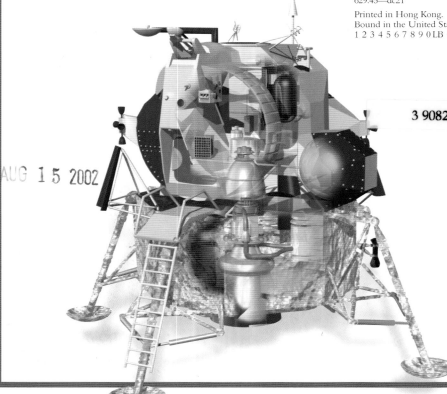

AUG 1 5 2002

3 9082 08878 1722

▶ Moon explorers return to Earth. They are dressed in special suits to keep humans safe from Moon germs.

CONTENTS

ROARING ROCKETS

The Moon is a long way from Earth, but at night it can seem very close. For thousands of years people looked up at the Moon and wondered what it would be like to go there. This book tells the story of how people finally found a way to travel there, and how a human first walked on the Moon.

▶ A German V-2 rocket, one of the first rocket-powered bombs, is launched during World War II.

SHOOTING SHELLS

In 1865, the French writer Jules Verne wrote a book called *From The Earth To The Moon*. He described how giant shells could be fired to the Moon from a huge cannon. The shells would contain the first Moon explorers (see opposite).

This 1934 space suit does not look comfortable or safe! It was never tested in space.

In the 1930s, scientists in Germany, the United States (U.S.), and the Soviet Union started carrying out experiments with rockets. The first rockets were not very powerful. They could only reach heights of six hundred feet.

During World War II, from 1939 to 1945, people found a new use for rockets. Germany began making rockets that could travel for hundreds of miles. They used them to launch bombs at England.

After World War II, the German scientists who had made these deadly rockets went to work in the U.S. But for a long time the Americans did not realize just how important rockets would become.

An illustration from Jules Verne's book *From The Earth To The Moon.*

DAREDEVIL DOG

During the 1950s, there were two countries that were much more powerful than the rest. These were the U.S. and the Soviet Union (now Russia). They were so powerful that they were known as superpowers.

The two superpowers were great enemies. They competed with each other in weapons, politics, sports, and science. They also began an amazing space race to see who could explore the farthest in space.

▲ Laika the Soviet space dog in her capsule, not long before she became the first living creature in space.

SPUTNIK SPOTTERS

Many American children became *Sputnik* spotters. They stared into the sky at night and tried to spot the Soviet Union's satellites as they passed overhead.

▶ **This is a drawing of the Soviet Union's *Sputnik 1* satellite.**

In October 1957, the Soviet Union launched the world's first satellite, called *Sputnik*. A satellite is a machine that flies through space, traveling around Earth in a big loop, or orbit. *Sputnik* flew over the U.S. once every hour. Americans were terrified. They thought the Soviet Union might attack them from space.

Soon the Soviet Union was even farther ahead in the space race. It launched *Sputnik 2*, a satellite containing a female dog named Laika. She spent ten days in orbit around Earth. The Soviet Union was the first country to put a living creature in space.

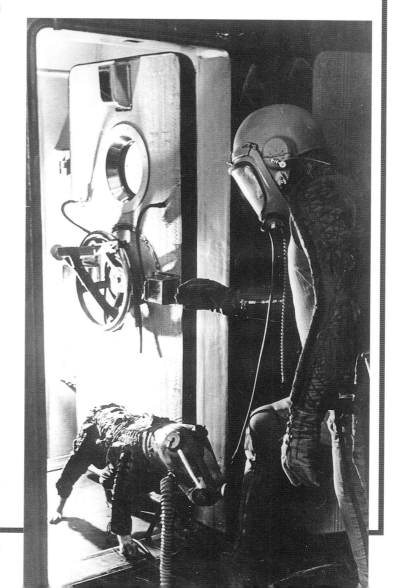

▶ **Russian astronauts with their space dog, testing out their space suits.**

MERCURY MAGIC

The U.S. tried to launch its own satellite called *Explorer* in December 1957. The launch was a disaster. The rocket that was supposed to fire the satellite into space exploded before it left the ground!

▲ The seven Mercury astronauts in their space suits.

The U.S. was a long way behind in the space race. Then two things happened. An organization called NASA was formed to run the U.S. space projects. Also, John F. Kennedy became President of the U.S. Kennedy gave NASA a goal. He said it should land a man on the Moon and return him safely to Earth by 1970.

▼ President Kennedy calls for the U.S. to send a man to the Moon by 1970.

◄ Magazines like this one are very popular with space enthusiasts.

NASA began the Mercury Project, with the aim of getting a human into space. Seven astronauts were chosen to fly spacecraft for the project, and they quickly became heroes. People thought the astronauts were very brave, and they wanted to know everything about them. The seven men appeared on television, and in newspapers and magazines. Americans were becoming more and more interested in space.

SPACE CRAZE

By the early 1960s, the U.S. had gone crazy about space. There were space programs on television, space records in the music charts, and even space coloring books!

▲ *Explorer I*, moments before it exploded on the launch pad.

SPACEMAN

SHEPARD'S DELIGHT

A month after Gagarin's success, the American astronaut Alan Shepard made a short flight in a spacecraft called *Freedom 7*. But he traveled only about 280 miles (450 km), and his spacecraft did not travel all around Earth.

The Soviet Union began sending up spacecraft called probes to take photographs of the Moon in 1959. Probes send back information automatically, so they do not need anybody on board. But the Soviet Union also had plans to send a man into space.

▼ The launch of *Vostok I* from Baykonur in the Soviet Union at 9:07 A.M. on April 12, 1961. The astronaut Yuri Gagarin was on board.

On April 12, 1961, a spacecraft called *Vostok I* was launched from the Soviet Union. An astronaut named Yuri Gagarin was on board. He flew 203 miles (327 km) above Earth's surface and into space. Gagarin circled the world before landing back in the Soviet Union.

In the U.S., people were shocked when they heard about Gagarin's flight. The Soviet Union had won everything so far in the space race. It had launched the first satellite and put the first living creature in space. Now, it had put the first human in space. There was only one race left to win. That was the race to put a human on the Moon.

▲ Celebrations in the Soviet Union after Yuri Gagarin became the first man to visit space.

▶ Alan Shepard after his return to Earth, with the *Freedom 7* capsule behind him.

11

SPACE WALK

The U.S. had some catching up to do in the space race. It began an important program called the Gemini Project.

The Gemini Project had three goals. First, an astronaut had to make a space walk, by going outside the spacecraft during a flight. Second, astronauts had to show they could stay alive in space for a long time. Third, two spacecraft had to link up, or dock, in space. If they could do these three things, the Americans believed they would be almost ready to send a human to the Moon and back.

▲ America's *Gemini 6* spacecraft about to dock with *Gemini 7*. To dock they would join spacecraft together in space.

WOLF WALK

The first ever space walk was made by Soviet astronaut Alexei A. Leonov in March 1965. But when his spacecraft, *Voskhod 2*, returned to Earth, it landed in a lonely forest. Leonov had to fight off hungry wolves before he was rescued!

In June 1966, astronaut Ed White left a spacecraft called *Gemini 4* and made a space walk. The project's next spacecraft, *Gemini 5*, orbited Earth 120 times. This was the longest spaceflight yet. It showed that humans could stay alive in space. Finally, the spacecraft *Gemini 6* and *Gemini 7* docked while in orbit. The Gemini Project had achieved its goals.

▲ Astronaut Ed White floats in space during his space walk. He used a rocket gun to move himself forward.

AMAZING APOLLO

NASA started to make plans for the journey to the Moon. It began a project called Apollo. The aim of the Apollo Project was to build a spacecraft that could carry a human safely to the Moon and back.

▼ NASA planned to land astronauts on the Moon in a lunar module.

Moon

Command module orbits Moon

After orbiting Earth, command module and lunar module head toward Moon

Rocket takes off and separates

Earth

Lunar module lands on Moon

NASA came up with a special plan. A giant rocket would send the spacecraft toward the Moon. As it used up its fuel, parts of the rocket would fall away. Finally, only two parts of the spacecraft would be left. One part, called the lunar module, would land on the Moon. The other part, called the command module, would stay in orbit around the Moon. Then it would dock with the lunar module and carry the astronauts safely back to Earth.

APOLLO TRAGEDY

The Apollo Project had a very bad start. The first spacecraft, *Apollo I*, began practicing its launch, or takeoff. Suddenly there was an explosion. The three astronauts on board were all killed in this tragic accident.

▲ *Apollo 9's* lunar module docks with the command module in 1968.

Scientists began building a giant rocket, named *Saturn 5*. It was tested in November 1967. This would carry the Apollo spacecraft into space. Work also began on a lunar module that could land safely on the Moon. The U.S. was almost ready to send an astronaut to the Moon.

INTO ORBIT

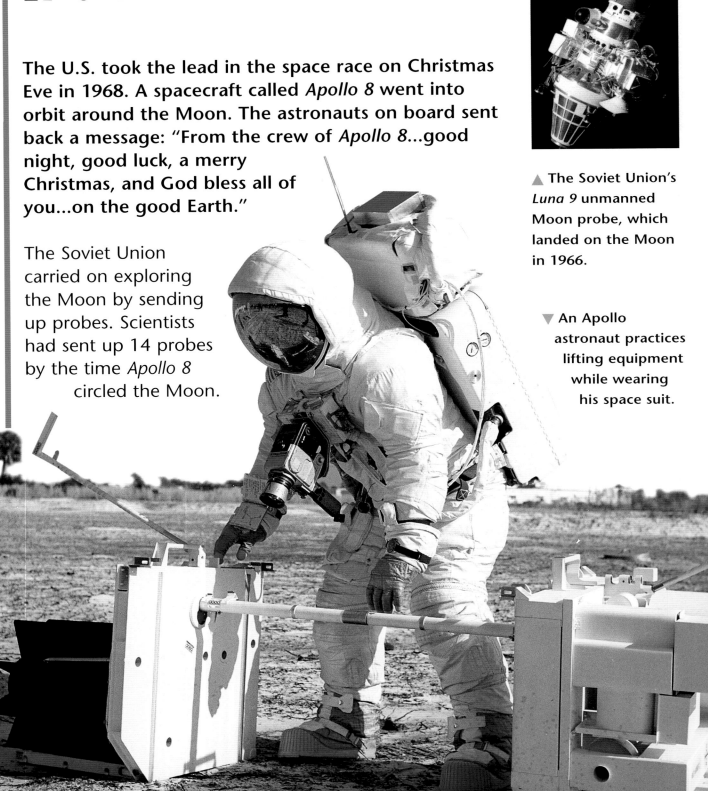

The U.S. took the lead in the space race on Christmas Eve in 1968. A spacecraft called *Apollo 8* went into orbit around the Moon. The astronauts on board sent back a message: "From the crew of *Apollo 8*...good night, good luck, a merry Christmas, and God bless all of you...on the good Earth."

The Soviet Union carried on exploring the Moon by sending up probes. Scientists had sent up 14 probes by the time *Apollo 8* circled the Moon.

▲ The Soviet Union's *Luna 9* unmanned Moon probe, which landed on the Moon in 1966.

▼ An Apollo astronaut practices lifting equipment while wearing his space suit.

Some of the probes landed on the Moon. Others passed by and went on into space. The probes gathered lots of information, but still no human had stood on the Moon's surface.

The American spacecraft *Apollo 9* and *Apollo 10* both carried a lunar module into space for tests in March and May of 1969. When they came back to Earth, their astronauts reported that the module worked perfectly. Everything was now ready for *Apollo 11* to make the first landing on the Moon.

▼ *Apollo 9's* **command module in orbit around Earth.**

MARVELOUS MARBLE

The *Apollo 8* astronauts were the first people to see Earth from space. It must be strange to see your own planet from such a distance. One of the astronauts said it looked like a "big, blue marble."

LUNAR LANDING

Early in the morning of July 16, 1969, *Apollo 11* took off from Cape Canaveral in Florida. On board were the astronauts Neil Armstrong, Buzz Aldrin, and Mike Collins. Over a million people were gathered at Cape Canaveral to watch as the massive rocket blasted off. Millions more saw the liftoff on television.

MOTOR MOUTH

Scientists kept an eye on *Apollo 11* from a center in Houston, Texas, called Mission Control. During the Moon landing, the astronauts were talked to by a man at Mission Control called Charlie Duke. He talked so much that someone nudged him and said: "Shut up and let them land!"

▶ *Apollo 11* blasts off from its launch pad at Cape Canaveral, Florida.

Apollo 11 took three days to travel to the Moon. When it arrived, Armstrong and Aldrin climbed into the lunar module, which was called *Eagle*. Collins pushed a button inside the command module, and the *Eagle* broke away. Armstrong and Aldrin were on their way to the surface of the Moon.

Close to the surface, Armstrong looked down at where they had planned to land. He saw that it was too rocky. The *Eagle's* fuel was running out. But Armstrong flew on, searching for a good landing spot. At the last moment, he saw one. *Eagle* landed with its fuel tanks nearly empty.

▼ The lunar module *Eagle*, separated from the command module, floats above the surface of the Moon.

A Giant Leap

Millions of people watched on televisions around the world as Neil Armstrong opened the door of the *Eagle*. For thousands of years, people had looked up at the Moon and wondered what it would be like to stand on it. Now, they were about to find out.

▲ Buzz Aldrin comes out of *Eagle* and begins to climb down the ladder to the surface of the Moon.

◄ Armstrong, Aldrin, and the American flag stand in the sunlight on the Moon.

▼ Buzz Aldrin setting up an experiment on the Moon.

Armstrong stepped through the door, and climbed down *Eagle's* ladder. Then, he put one foot on the surface of the Moon and said, "That's one small step for man, one giant leap for mankind."

Aldrin joined Armstrong on the Moon shortly afterward. Gravity, the force that keeps our feet on the ground, is six times weaker on the Moon than it is on Earth. So the astronauts felt very light. They were able to take giant steps, covering 7 feet (2 m) in a single leap!

The astronauts took out an American flag and planted it on the Moon's surface. This was the moment the U.S. had been waiting for. Their flag, and not that of the Soviet Union, was the first to be placed there. They had won the race to the Moon!

FANTASTIC FOOTPRINTS

As they walked around, the astronauts made footprints in the dusty surface of the Moon. There is no air on the Moon to blow the dust away, so these footprints will last for thousands of years!

SPLASHDOWN!

Apollo 11 returned to Earth on July 24, 1969. The spacecraft entered Earth's atmosphere at a speed of 24,700 mph (39,750 kmh). Because it was traveling so fast, it was glowing with heat!

▼ The three astronauts being taken from the command module after splashdown.

Parachutes opened to slow *Apollo 11* down. By the time it hit the surface of the Pacific Ocean, it was moving much more slowly. The astronauts had traveled 497,000 miles (800,000 km). They made their splashdown just 12 miles (20 km) from the ship that was to pick them up.

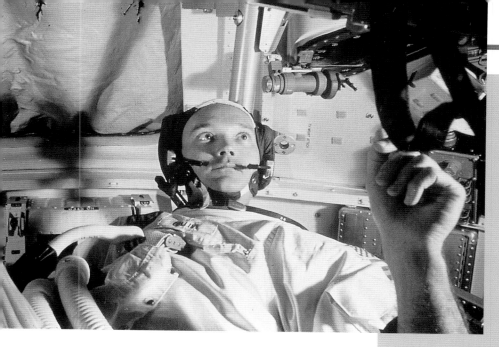

Mike Collins in the command module.

ALL ALONE

The pilot of the command module, Mike Collins, never walked on the Moon. But he did some special things of his own. As he traveled around the Moon, he spent time all alone on its far side. He was farther from Earth than any other person.

President Nixon was waiting to greet the astronauts. But he was not allowed to shake their hands. Scientists were worried that the astronauts might have brought a horrible Moon disease back to Earth with them!

Armstrong, Aldrin, and Collins became heroes across America. This photo shows a parade for them in New York City.

The astronauts were kept away from everyone for three weeks. When they were allowed out, they found that they had become heroes. Parties and parades were held to celebrate the amazing achievement of the first humans on the Moon.

SPACE STATION

▼ The space shuttle is used to carry astronauts and equipment to the International Space Station.

The amazing race had been won. Humans had reached the Moon. But *Apollo 11* was not the last spacecraft to carry people to the Moon.

Between 1969 and 1972, Apollo spacecraft carried astronauts to the Moon six times. In 1972, the final mission to the Moon, *Apollo 17,* left a plaque on the Moon's surface. It read: "Here man completed his first explorations of the Moon, December 1972." No human has stood on the Moon since.

▼ The American space shuttle docks with the Russian space station *Mir*.

▲ The International
Space Station

But people have not stopped exploring space. Scientists still send probes to distant planets. They also build huge spacecraft called space stations, such as the International Space Station, where astronauts can live and work for months at a time.

But the Soviet Union and the U.S. no longer fight over space. Instead, different countries work together to study the amazing moons, stars, and planets of space.

SUPER STATION

The largest project in space is the International Space Station. This huge structure allows Russia (part of the former Soviet Union), the U.S. and 14 other countries to work together. Scientists will carry out experiments in the space station that are impossible to do on Earth.

▲ U.S. Senator John Glenn, one of America's first astronauts, before he returned to space in 1998.

SPACE RACE FACTS

Unlucky brake
Yuri Gagarin became the first man in space in 1961. But in 1995 secret notes about his flight were found. They showed that his spacecraft almost crashed on its way back to Earth, because of a problem with its braking rocket.

First females
After his amazing flight, Yuri Gagarin went on to become the training director of the first-ever program to train female astronauts.

Space professor
Neil Armstrong earned his pilot's license on his 16th birthday! He later worked as a fighter-pilot. When he retired from NASA in 1971, he became a professor of engineering at the University of Cincinnati.

Monkey business
Scientists were worried that humans would not be able to stay alive when traveling in a rocket at amazing speeds. So, between 1948 and 1952, scientists in the U.S. carried out tests. They flew monkeys on rockets that had been captured from Germany.

Star laws
There are many laws in space. One of the most important is the 1967 Outer Space Treaty. This says that the Moon and all other moons, stars, and planets are free to be explored by people from all countries.

◀ Wernher von Braun, one of the first rocket scientists.

Rocket man

Many of the scientists who worked on rockets for the U.S. after World War II came from Germany. Wernher von Braun, one of the most important scientists, had worked on the building of rocket-powered bombs for the German leader Adolf Hitler.

Mighty *Mir*

In 1986, the Soviet Union launched a space station called *Mir,* which means "peace" in Russian. *Mir* finally came back to Earth in March 2001, after 14 years in space.

Good Goddard!

The first rockets launched in the U.S. were built by a famous American named Robert Goddard. He was once asked by the State of Massachusetts not to set off his rockets within the state. The rockets were thought to be too dangerous!

Rocket to riches

In 1960, the widow of Robert Goddard accepted $1,000,000. In return, the U.S. government was allowed to use the rockets he had invented in its space program.

▶ Valentina Tereshkova, who became the first woman in space in 1963.

Valentina's day

The first woman in space was Valentina Tereshkova. She traveled into space on June 16, 1963, on a spacecraft called *Vostok 6*. She returned to Earth three days later.

Shuttle Ride

The U.S. did not get a woman into space until 20 years after the Soviets! The first American woman in space was Sally Ride, who flew aboard the space shuttle in 1983.

Space Race Words

Apollo (uh-POL-loh)
Apollo was the third program set up by the U.S. to explore space. The *Apollo 11* spacecraft carried the first people to reach the Moon.

astronaut (AS-truh-nawt)
Someone who travels into space.

atmosphere (AT-muhss-fihr)
The group of gases around the surface of a planet. Close to Earth's surface, the atmosphere is made up mainly of nitrogen. Higher up, there are other gases such as ozone.

automatically (aw-tuh-MAT-ik-uh-lee)
Working by itself, without the need for human control. Space probes travel and automatically send back information, such as recordings and photographs. So they do not need a pilot.

▶ The *Eagle* lunar module.

command module (kuh-MAND MOJ-ool)
The part of an Apollo spacecraft that stayed in orbit around the Moon while the lunar module visited the Moon's surface.

dock (dok)
Join spacecraft together in space.

Gemini (JEM-in-nye)
Gemini was the second program set up by the U.S. to explore space. The first American space walk was made from a spacecraft called *Gemini 4*.

gravity (GRAV-uh-tee)
Any object has a natural force called gravity, that pulls things toward it.

The gravity of Earth is what holds us all on the ground and stops us from floating off into space!

liftoff
The moment when a rocket leaves the ground, also called blastoff.

lunar (LOO-nur)
Lunar simply means anything to do with the Moon.

lunar module (LOO-nur MOJ-ool)
The part of an Apollo spacecraft that visited the surface of the Moon and then brought the astronauts back to the command module.

Mercury (MUR-kyuh-ree)
Mercury was the first program set up by the U.S. to explore space.

Mission Control (MISH-uhn)
The American command center on Earth that runs space flights. For the Apollo space flights, Mission Control was in Houston, Texas.

NASA (NAS-suh)
NASA stands for National Aeronautics and Space Agency, and was formed in the U.S. in 1958. Before NASA existed, both the U.S. Army and the U.S. Navy had their own rocket programs. NASA combined these programs, and helped the U.S. to catch up with the Soviet Union in the space race.

▲ The *Skylab* space station orbiting Earth.

orbit (OR-bit)
The path that a smaller object travels through space around a larger one. For example, the Moon travels in orbit around Earth. The Moon is held in this orbit by the pull of gravity from Earth. Spacecraft such as satellites can also be sent into orbit around moons, stars, and planets.

politics (POL-uh-tiks)
Different ways of running countries and forming governments.

probe (prohb)
A spacecraft without anyone on board that explores distant moons and planets. Both the U.S. and the Soviet Union have sent many probes into space. Some are still traveling through space today, sending back information about the objects they pass.

rocket (ROK-it)
A powerful engine that burns fuel, and releases a jet of gas that moves the engine forward very quickly. Rockets are used to carry bombs and spacecraft to their target. Powerful rockets are needed to fire spacecraft away from the pull of Earth's gravity.

satellite (SAT-uh-lite)
A satellite is a machine that flies through space, traveling around a large object, such as Earth or the Moon in a big loop, or orbit.

space station (STAY-shuhn)
A large satellite in space, on which astronauts can live and work for long periods of time.

Sputnik **(SPUT-nik)**
Sputnik means "traveling companion" in Russian. It was the name given to three satellites from the Soviet Union launched in 1957–1958.

superpower (SOO-pur POW-ur)
A superpower is a country that is much more powerful than most other countries. During the space race, the Soviet Union and the U.S. were known as the world's two superpowers.

Soviet Union (SOH-vee-et YOON-yuhn)
A huge country in eastern Europe, which was formed in 1922 with Russia at its heart. In 1991, the Soviet Union broke up into much smaller states.

SPACE RACE PROJECTS

▶ The Moon, seen from space.

MOON LANDING REPORT

Write a newspaper article about the Moon landing. To write your report, use the information in this book and in other books and websites. You could write your report in one of three ways:

1. Pretend you are an American reporter. Write an article telling the people of the U.S. how two Americans have just become the first people on the Moon.

2. Pretend you are a news reporter from the Soviet Union. Your job is to tell people how the Americans have landed on the Moon. But you must also remind them of all the things the Soviet Union has done in space.

3. Imagine you are an alien visiting from another galaxy.

What do you think of the Moon landing? Remember that such a visitor would have traveled from a lot farther away than the Moon!

MOON SPOTTER

Try to find a book that includes a map of the Moon. You might be able to find one that shows the different areas where the Moon landings took place. You can also look on the Internet to see if there are any maps of the Moon.

Now you need a telescope! Your school might have one. There might even be a local club for astronomers, people who like to study the stars. Ask about these things at your school. On a clear night and using a telescope, you can actually see some of the different areas where the Moon landings took place.

SPACE RACE ON THE INTERNET

If you can get onto the Internet, you will be able to track down some more information about the space race. Try looking up these websites to start you off:

NASA website
www.nasa.gov

Some of the best websites about space belong to NASA. Among them is a site where you can read the information that was given to newspapers before the *Apollo 11* mission. This might be useful if you have chosen to be an American reporter for the Moon landing report project.

Kennedy Space Center
www.ksc.nasa.gov

The Kennedy Space Center is where the Apollo flights were launched. This website has pages on the history of the space program and tells about what is happening at the center today.

NASA Human Spaceflight
www.spaceflight.nasa.gov

The International Space Center homepage is also the homepage for the space shuttle.

▶ Buzz Aldrin walking on the Moon.

The Space Museum
www.spacerace.8m.com

Features quotes concerning the space race, as well as some great pictures.

You can search for other sites on the space race using any search engine. Try typing in keywords such as "rocket," "Gemini," or "Apollo."

INDEX

© Belitha Press Ltd. 2002